To all the students who have written to me over the past
twenty-five years, I am extremely grateful for your trust in me.
You are the inspiration for this book — I heard your hearts.
— RB

For Mihoko and Maya.
My journey through this book is a reminder
of the loving support of my family.
— JJC

"Don't follow the path. Go where there is no path and
begin the trail. When you start a new trail equipped
with courage, strength, and conviction, the only
thing that can stop you is you!"

— Ruby Bridges

All rights reserved. Published by Orchard Books, an imprint of Scholastic Inc., *Publishers since 1920*. ORCHARD BOOKS and design are registered trademarks of Watts Publishing Group, Ltd., used under license. SCHOLASTIC and associated logos are trademarks and/or registered trademarks of Scholastic Inc. • The publisher does not have any control over and does not assume any responsibility for author or third-party websites or their content. • No part of this publication may be reproduced, stored in a retrieval system, or transmitted in any form or by any means, electronic, mechanical, photocopying, recording, or otherwise, without written permission of the publisher. For information regarding permission, write to Scholastic Inc., Attention: Permissions Department, 557 Broadway, New York, NY 10012.

The letters in *Dear Ruby, Hear Our Hearts* are real, but the illustrations have been imagined by the artist to protect the students' identities.

Library of Congress Cataloging-in-Publication Data available

ISBN 978-1-338-75391-2

10 9 8 7 6 5 4 3 2 1   24 25 26 27 28

Printed in China 62   First edition, January 2024

Book design by Patti Ann Harris and Rae Crawford
The text type was set in Bodoni 72 Oldstyle and KG Burst My Bubble.
The display type was set in Chaplet and KG Summer Storm Rough.
The artwork for this book was drawn entirely with wax pencils and brushes of ink and colored digitally.

Letters to Civil Rights Activist RUBY BRIDGES

DEAR RUBY,
hear our hearts

BY
RUBY BRIDGES

ILLUSTRATIONS BY
JOHN JAY CABUAY

ORCHARD BOOKS
An Imprint of Scholastic Inc. • New York

THE
RUBY BRIDGES
FOUNDATION

Dear Reader,

The inspiration for *Dear Ruby, Hear Our Hearts* came from the thousands of letters I have received from students over the past twenty-five years of my journey visiting schools across America.

Like my six-year-old self, these students had ideas and concerns that ran deeper than we grown-ups gave them credit for.

I've heard their hearts and now share those hearts with you. These pages truly speak to the power of children!

Enjoy,
Ruby Bridges

A POEM FOR RUBY

I am not a mouse.

Mice are skittish and scared.

I am a lion roaring to the sky,

a cheetah running as fast as the wind,

an orca jumping out of

　　the deep

　　　　dark

　　　　　ocean.

I am not a mouse.

　　　　by Liesl

BE BRAVE!

Dear Ruby,

My name is Olivia. Thank you for sharing your story. It made me want to be brave and stand up to make a change. You showed me to not give up when something is unfair. You can make it change, no matter what. I bet you were scared just like me. You said that if someone or something is putting you down, you get back up.

My heart heard that, and I am trying to be more like you.

Sincerely,
Olivia

My dearest Olivia,

I am so pleased you wrote to me, especially about standing up. I know all too well how scary it can be to stand up for yourself or even others. Just know it takes a courageous and brave person to stand up even if you are afraid. It happens to us all!

I am proud of you,
Ruby Bridges

DON'T BULLY ME!

Dear Ruby,

My name is Tala. I have learned a lot about you in class and thought it was so brave of you to go to an all-white school. You have inspired me in so many ways. As the smallest person in class, I have learned from you that it is okay if you are different or unique.

Sometimes kids bully me because I am smaller than most people in my grade, but when I think about your bravery, I think I can be brave, too.

I hope you have a great day!

Sincerely,
Tala

Dear Tala,

Thanks for sharing your thoughts with me. It took a long time for me to learn just how special I am, and I am so happy I know now. Yes, it's okay to be different because what really matters is your heart and what's inside! Remember that!

Stay strong,
Ruby Bridges

Dear Ruby,

I am writing to you because you know what it is like to be judged, and yet you have been brave your entire life. You have stood up against hatred in a kind way.

As an Asian girl, I feel sad and angry about this thing called "Asian Hate"! My family is being judged for how we look, and people are violent against us. It is important to stop violence because I want my family, and all families, to be safe.

I am using my art skills to stop violence. All I want is for this world to be a peaceful place for all people to live.

Once again, thank you for any help you can give us to keep us safe.

Love,
Melody

Dear Melody,

Your concerns about Asian Hate really bother me. It's also heartbreaking that all people don't understand just how unfair this behavior is. We all deserve to live happy, safe, and peaceful lives! I will help by continuing to speak out against all hatred and any form of racism.

Your friend,
Ruby Bridges

SAVE OUR PLANET!

Dear Ruby Bridges,

My name is Madison. Your story inspired individuals like me to achieve something brighter and better. When I grow up, I want to help the world by inventing artificial plants to reduce the carbon dioxide in our atmosphere. Carbon dioxide can cause damage to our climate by starting floods, storms, and other natural disasters.

Thank you for inspiring people of different backgrounds to try to achieve their goals and dreams. Your impact has changed the world.

Thank you for reading my letter.

In appreciation,
Madison

Dear Madison,

Your letter inspired me by how, at eleven years old, you're already thinking about the future of our planet. Clearly, this is a problem that is affecting and will continue to affect the well-being of us all. We need more young people such as yourself to be more conscientious about the planet and environment. I know your goals will definitely have a positive impact!

Continue to dream,
Ruby Bridges

HELP THE HOMELESS!

Dear Ms. Ruby,

My name is Keira. I want to make a difference by trying to get companies to know how much food they are throwing away — so much food.

It should be given to the homeless!

From,
Keira

Dear Keira,

I'm happy to receive your letter concerning homelessness. I agree with your idea of trying to get more companies to come up with plans to save food they are throwing away. We must not allow people to continue to go hungry. Being without a home is horrible enough; being hungry, too, seems horribly unjust.

"Feed the people!"
Ruby Bridges

CHALLENGES!

Dear Ms. Ruby Bridges,

Thank you for your hard work and bravery. You helped me see the world in a different way. Thank you for opening my eyes to racial inequality. School is hard for me, too. I know these problems personally, but not quite the same way you do.

The problem that I face has to do with my learning challenges. With my dyslexia, I get pulled out of many classes. I still have trouble writing. Dyslexia is really hard and annoying.

I hope you keep fighting the good fight, and I will, too.

Sincerely,
Emma

Dear Emma,

I appreciate your letter sharing your thoughts on the problems we have that concern you the most, such as learning challenges. It's hard to not be worried about these issues, but you are facing them, which is such a brave and positive thing to do. Now what others must do is work to find solutions to make learning work for all of us, because we all learn in different ways!

Continue to be brave and patient with yourself.

Sincerely,
Ruby Bridges

GIRLS RULE!

Dear Ms. Ruby Bridges,

Something I'm passionate about changing is girls' rights. I think that sometimes people can underestimate girls, like when it comes to certain sports or jobs. Girls can do the same things as boys or even better sometimes.

What I love to do is play football. Some people think that's just for boys, but I don't. I wonder why there is a boys' football team but not a girls' football team. I have met lots of girls who love football, but they say they're too scared or embarrassed to try out.

When I get to high school, I want to ask the principal to start a girls' team. And then hopefully we can try and convince other schools to make girls' football teams, too.

Then people might change their ideas of what girls can or can't do.

Sincerely,
Christina

Dear Christina,

It's great hearing from you and even better to know that we share some of the same passions: girls' rights and football. Unfortunately, yes, we still underestimate the power of the female in so many ways — even though I must admit we have made lots of great progress for women's rights since the Nineteenth Amendment granted women the right to vote in 1920. No doubt, with the help of young people such as yourself, soon we'll be able to say, "time to pass the football."

Press on,
Ruby Bridges

Dear Ruby Bridges,

You changed the world so much with your courage and bravery. Without you, I might not have the same friends I have today.

I hope I can help to change gun violence. Even though you can try to change kids' points of view about gun control, you still need to change adults' points of view. It's like some of them do not understand the importance of gun control.

If everyone had the courage you had, maybe my dream would come true.

Sincerely,
Ben

Dear Ben,

Thanks for writing, and I'm grateful for your faith in my efforts to make change in this world. Knowing that you are behind me and supporting me every step of the way gives me the hope that we can, one day, change the laws around gun rights! It won't be easy, but we must never give up trying!

"Keep the faith,"
Ruby Bridges

COURAGE TO BE ME!

Dear Ruby Bridges,

   You are a big leader, and I know now that I can stand up to anything because of you. Someone once said to me that I couldn't skate because I was fat. I was about to give up, but because of you, I practiced every weekend and now I am a very good skater.

   I was very anxious when I tried to stand up to people. But now that I have read more about your courage, I am not as fearful.

   Now every time I skate or think about being braver, I think of you and thank you.

                               Sincerely,
                               Taylor

My dearest Taylor,

   Thank you for sharing your thoughts with me! I must say, you have more courage than you think. It takes a lot to stand up to people that constantly put you down, but you did it!

   Now *that* is bravery! I'm so proud of you, especially when you said that my story inspired you. You can do anything when you set your mind to it!

                               Stay strong,
                               Ruby Bridges

GLOSSARY

anxious an·xious (**angk**-shuhs) *adjective* To feel worried or scared.

artificial ar·ti·fi·cial (ahr-tuh-**fish**-uhl) *adjective* Made by people rather than existing in nature.

atmosphere at·mo·sphere (**at**-muhs-feer) *noun* The mixture of gases that surrounds a planet.

bravery bra·ve·ry (**bray**-vuh-ree) *noun* If you face something with **bravery**, you face it with courage and determination.

carbon dioxide car·bon di·ox·ide (**car**-buhn dye-**ahk**-syde) *noun* A gas that is a mixture of carbon and oxygen, with no color or odor. People and animals breathe this gas out, while plants absorb it during the day.

challenges chal·len·ges (**chal**-en-jehs) *noun* Difficult things that require extra work or effort to do.

courageous cou·ra·geous (kuh-**ray**-juhs) *adjective* When you are **courageous**, you have the ability to do something that scares you.

dyslexia dys·lex·i·a (dis-**lek**-see-uh) *noun* A condition that makes it difficult to read, write, and distinguish letters properly or in the correct order.

environment en·vi·ron·ment (en-**vye**-ruhn-mehnt) *noun* All the things that are part of your life and have an effect on it, such as your family and your school, the place you live on Earth, and the events that happen to you.

fearful fear·ful (**feer**-full) *adjective* To be afraid of someone or something.

gun control gun con·trol (**gun** kun-troll) *noun* The regulation of the sale and use of firearms.

hatred hat·red (**hay**-trid) *noun* Intense dislike; the feeling of someone who hates.

impact im·pact (**im**-pakt) *noun* The force of impression of one thing on another; a significant or major effect.

inspired in·spi·red (in-**spy**-urd) *verb* To have influenced someone with an emotion, an idea, or an attitude.

inventing in·vent·ing (in-**vent**-ing) *verb* Designing or creating something.

natural disasters nat·u·ral dis·as·ters (**natch**-ur-uhl di-**zas**-turs) *noun* Natural events such as floods, earthquakes, or hurricanes that cause great damage or loss of life.

Nineteenth Amendment to the United States Constitution Nine·teenth A·mend·ment to the U·nit·ed States Con·sti·tu·tion (**nyne**-teenth uh-**mend**-ment too thuh yoo-**nite**-ed stayts kahn-stih-**too**-shun) *noun* "The right of citizens of the United States to vote shall not be denied or abridged by the United States or by any State on account of sex. Congress shall have power to enforce this article by appropriate legislation."

racial inequality ra·cial in·e·qual·i·ty (**ray**-shuhl in-e-**kwa**-li-tee) *noun* The unequal distribution of resources, power, and economic opportunity across race in a society.

rights rights (rites) *noun* If you have the **right** to do something, then you are legally or morally entitled to do it, as in the right to remain silent.

solutions so·lu·tions (suh-**loo**-shuhns) *noun* Answers to or means of solving problems, as in *simple solutions*.

underestimate un·der·es·ti·mate (uhn-dur-**es**-tuh-mate) *verb* To think that something is smaller, weaker, or less important than it really is.

violence vio·lence (**vye**-lints) *noun* The use of physical force to cause harm.

well-being well·be·ing (well-**bee**-ing) *noun* A state of being healthy and happy.

ABOUT THE LETTERS

Ruby Bridges has been traveling around the United States spreading her mission to end racism and all forms of bullying through integration and education for over twenty-five years. Ruby's vision is to generate tomorrow's leaders by fostering the compassion, confidence, and knowledge required to make a better world for all. Thousands of students sent letters to Ruby with their concerns and hopes for the future.